The sequel to the powerful memoir *Fatty Legs*

a stranger at home

A True Story

Christy JORDAN-FENTON *&*
Margaret POKIAK-FENTON

Artwork by Liz Amini-Holmes

annick press
toronto + new york + vancouver

J
B
JORDAN-FENTON C./
JOR

Annick Press Ltd.

Edited by Maggie de Vries
Copyedited by Pam Robertson
Proofread by Gillian Watts
Cover and interior design by Lisa Hemingway
Cover and interior illustrations by Liz Amini-Holmes

Cataloging in Publication
Jordan-Fenton, Christy
    A stranger at home: a true story / Christy Jordan-Fenton & Margaret Pokiak-Fenton ; artwork by Liz Amini-Holmes.
Sequel to: Fatty legs.
ISBN 978-1-55451-362-8 (bound).—ISBN 978-1-55451-361-1 (pbk.)

1. Pokiak-Fenton, Margaret—Childhood and youth—Juvenile literature. 2. Inuit—Canada—Residential schools—Juvenile literature. 3. Inuit women—Biography—Juvenile literature. I. Pokiak-Fenton, Margaret II. Amini-Holmes, Liz III. Title.

E96.5.J652 2011   J371.829'9712071   C2011-902079-3

We acknowledge the support of the Canada Council for the Arts, the Ontario Arts Council, and the Government of Canada through the Canada Book Fund (CBF) for our publishing activities.

ONTARIO ARTS COUNCIL
CONSEIL DES ARTS DE L'ONTARIO

Printed and bound in China.

Published in the U.S.A. by
Annick Press (U.S.) Ltd.

Distributed in Canada by
Firefly Books Ltd.
66 Leek Crescent
Richmond Hill, ON
L4B 1H1

Distributed in the U.S.A. by
Firefly Books (U.S.) Inc.
P.O. Box 1338
Ellicott Station
Buffalo, NY 14205

VISIT OUR WEBSITE AT WWW.ANNICKPRESS.COM
VISIT LIZ AMINI-HOLMES AT WWW.LUNAVILLA.COM

FOR MY THREE LITTLE INSPIRATIONS—Qugyuk, Aklak, and Paniktuaq—and their loving father, my husband, Garth: without your patience yet again, this book would not have been possible. For Margaret: your courage continues to be an inspiration to all who know you. And for Keith, a keeper of the fire: thank you for sharing a flame of inspiration with me. Megwich.

— *Christy*

TO CHRISTY: I am so grateful for all the time and care you have put into these books. To my children, and everyone else who has stood behind me in this: thank you for all the support you have given me. And, as always, to my late husband, Lyle, whose love and never-ending support helped me to overcome. He was a great man.

— *Margaret*

FOR MY MOST WONDROUS CREATIONS, Alek and Max, and my loving and talented husband, Mark, all of whom are my wellspring of inspiration, strength, and encouragement. To Diana, now the brightest star among the Northern Lights. And to Christy, Margaret, and Annick Press, who paid me the highest compliment by allowing me illustrate these tender and important stories.

— *Liz*

Margaret with her sisters Mabel and Bessie and their
mother, sitting in front of the smokehouse.

Introduction

M Y NAME IS OLEMAUN Pokiak—that's
OO-*lee-mawn.* Such a name probably sounds
strange to you. I can understand, because there was
a time in my life when it sounded strange to me, too.
Would you believe that at one point I could scarcely
remember my own name or even speak the same
language as my mother? Well, it's true. The outsiders
had locked my tongue with the spell of their "educa-
tion." But I was named for a stone that sharpens a
knife, and I was strong. I could not be worn down.

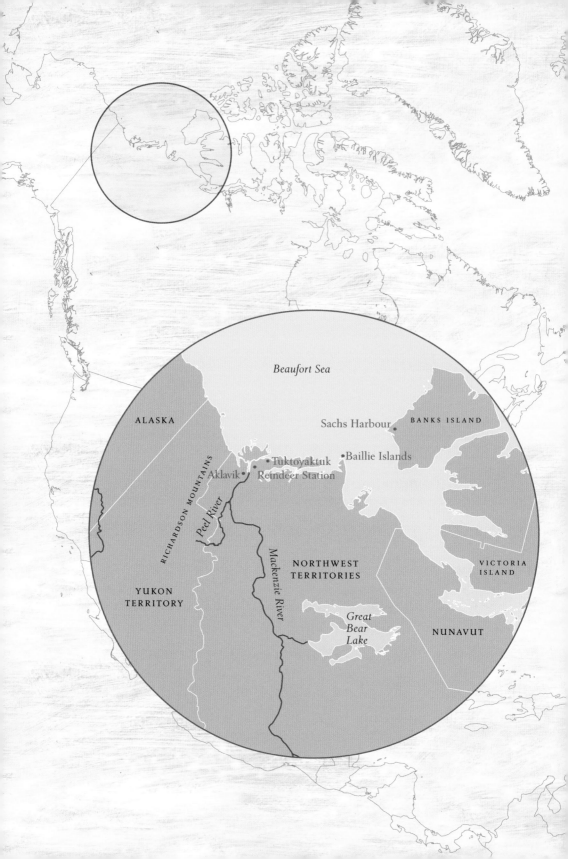

Beaufort Sea

ALASKA

Sachs Harbour   BANKS ISLAND

• Baillie Islands

Tuktoyaktuk
Aklavik • Reindeer Station

RICHARDSON MOUNTAINS

Peel River

Mackenzie River

NORTHWEST
TERRITORIES

VICTORIA
ISLAND

YUKON
TERRITORY

Great
Bear
Lake

NUNAVUT

Chapter ONE

THE BOAT CRUNCHED to a stop against the shore. My fingers gripped into the side of it as I propelled my body over the edge. "No," I heard my friend Agnes call with a restrained cry. The shore was packed with people, though Tuktoyaktuk was very small. I pushed through the crowd, my canvas shoes rolling on the tiny pebbles as I searched for my family. It had been so long since I had seen them.

I HEARD A VOICE I recognized—it was my mother's. She was speaking to my siblings. I turned and followed it, making my way through the throng to where she stood, with my two-year-old brother Ernest tied to her back and my sisters Mabel and Elizabeth still looking up at the boat for me to disembark. I wondered why my father had not run to meet me the minute my feet hit the shore, but he was not with them. I stood proudly before my mother and siblings and waited for them to rush toward me.

My mother gave me a strange look, as if to question why I was standing before her. I smiled, but she crossed her arms and shook her head. "Not my girl. Not *my* girl," she shouted up to the dark-cloaked brothers in the only English I had ever heard her speak.

See photo
on page 110.

I turned around to look at them where they stood, perched like birds of prey at the rail of the *Immaculata*. Their beady eyes studied me. If my mother didn't recognize me, I was certain that at any moment they would pounce on me and carry me back to their outsiders' nest up the Mackenzie Delta.

I could not understand how this could be happening. After days of being cramped aboard the small Roman Catholic boat, going ashore to stretch our legs only when we stopped to drop my classmates at their various Arctic settlements, this could not be my welcome. I had seen many mothers cry, and several fathers turn their heads to hide their own tears, as they welcomed back their children. After being gone for two years myself, I had all but lost hope that this day would come for me. But as each child left the boat on our way farther and farther north, my optimism grew. It grew until we reached the mouth of the Mackenzie River and then the hope inside of me erupted. The boat could barely contain the overwhelming anticipation I shared with my classmates. We had all waited for so long to be reunited with our parents in Tuktoyaktuk. Only my friend Agnes did not seem to be excited.

See photo on page 110.

When the shore came into view, its long, thin peninsula stretching out to meet us, I felt so happy I was sure I could walk on water like Jesus had in the nuns' stories. Not even Agnes's reluctance or the brothers' glares were enough to suppress the loud cheers that rose from the rest of us. The banks swelled with people, perhaps double the hundred or so who lived in Tuk most of the time. Like mine, other families had come from afar to collect their children. The trapper's daughter saw her father in the crowd and hugged her older brother, crying for joy. They had been gone just as long as I had been—two years. A short summer the year before had left many of us locked in by the ocean ice, with our parents unable to make it all the way to Aklavik to pick us up, or to arrange to get us from Tuk. The two older Gwich'in girls jumped up and down and waved to their family on the shore. The one named Katherine, who had always tried to bully me at school, was the happiest, because she was now thirteen and the outsiders could never make her go back to their school.

I wasn't going back either. I was going to tell my parents how awful the school was, so they would never make me leave the safety of our home on Banks Island ever again.

Now, on the shore, I looked from my unwelcoming mother up to where Agnes still stood on the deck of

Gwich'in: A tribe of the Dene Nation who live in the far northwestern part of Canada. The Gwich'in and the Inuvialuit have been known to feud with each other over resources.

the boat. She offered me a look of sympathy. Her own return had been painful the year before when she had gone home to Tuk for summer break.

I turned again to my mother. Our eyes were level; I was no longer the little girl who had always looked up at her. I was desperate to find a glint of recognition. There was none. Her face was still scrunched in protest, disbelieving that I was her child.

"Not my girl. Not my girl," she called again to the brothers. I looked again to the boat behind me where the brothers stood, and I tensed, ready to run if they made a move to come down and haul me away from my family. I was going to bolt. I'd run to the end of the peninsula and jump in the ocean if I had to. I was not returning to the school with them. I was never going to let them take me back.

It was their fault that my mother did not know me. It was because of the brothers, the priests, and the nuns that she could no longer see who I was. They had cast an outsiders' spell on me with their endless chores and poor meals; they had turned me from the plump, round-faced girl my mother knew into a skinny, gaunt creature. And they had cut my long black hair into a short, choppy bob. They had spent two years making all these changes. I was now ten, and several inches taller than I had been when my parents left me at that school up the river in Aklavik.

I scanned the crowd for my father. He had to come and save me! One of the brothers stepped onto the gangplank, and I leaned forward to run, but I was saved. My father emerged from the crowd and caught me in a tight embrace, the smoky smell of his parka wrapping around me. His strong hunter's hands stroked my hair.

"Olemaun," he said to me, the special name I had not heard for two years.

I whispered it to myself, "Oo-lee-maun."

The Inuit name my grandfather had given me felt strange to my tongue. I could not remember the last time I had thought of the name, let alone heard it spoken lovingly in my ear. I no longer felt worthy of it. It was like a beautiful dress that was far too big for me to wear. At the school I was known only as Margaret. Margaret was like a tight, scratchy dress, too

Inuit: a general term for the Aboriginal peoples who inhabit the Arctic regions of Canada, Greenland, Russia, and the United States. The term "Inuit" has largely replaced "Eskimo."

See photos on page 111.

small, like my school uniform. Not wanting my father to see that I was no longer his Olemaun, I buried my head against his chest.

I felt a soft touch, lighter than my father's, on my back. A familiar warm touch that worked its way into my heart with a tenderness I had not known for a long, long time. Only one person had ever touched me so sweetly—my mother. She slid her hand from my back and around my chest, reaching for my buried face. Her fingers were smooth against my chin. I shrank from them, filled with shame at having all but forgotten how affectionate a touch could be, and cried until my tears turned my father's parka wet.

My eight-year-old sister Elizabeth approached us first, while seven-year-old Mabel hung back. Then they joined us in a crushing hug, squeezing me in their embrace. Ernest reached out and touched my hair. All of those raven-eyed brothers together could not have pried me from my family. I was safe. By the time we separated, the brothers were pushing the *Immaculata* off the shore. They were moving on.

Katherine and the other Gwich'in girl would soon

be leaving too. The supply barge had been in Aklavik when we left and it would arrive here in Tuk any day. After that, Katherine would go with her people, far to the southwest of Tuk, and I would never have to see her again.

The trapper's daughter and her brother would also be going. As I watched their mother kiss them, I wondered how they felt about the school. Being outsiders like the nuns and the priests, they had not found the school so hard, but I could tell by the way they clung to their mother that they had missed her, just as I had missed my own family. I caught Agnes's eye and she smiled at me, waving good-bye as she supported her mother as they walked up the bank and toward the tiny village of log cabins and tent homes. I hoped I would get another chance to see her before the barge arrived and I left with my family for our distant island.

My mother assumed I would be hungry after my long journey down the Delta, so she had brought along a package of all my favorite things. I couldn't wait to eat my mother's food, but when we settled on the beach and she unwrapped the package, I nearly lost my

Muktuk

stomach. I was sickened by the pungent smell of whale blubber—muktuk, I remembered—the salty smell of dried fish, and the musky, gamey smell of meat and whipped caribou fat, which the outsiders called Eskimo ice cream, but it was nothing at all like ice cream. I crinkled my nose shut. The food smelled even worse than the swampy cabbage and disgusting bland, mushy porridge and beans we had to eat at the school.

My mother scrunched her brow and frowned. I could see how hurt she was that I was not eager to eat the food she had prepared for me.

At school we had been taught to pray before we ate, so I knew that God wanted me to drop to my knees to give thanks for the food I was about to receive, even though I was not so thankful for it. My family's eyes were on me, though, and I could not find the courage to pray in front of all of them. I made a note to give thanks later when I was alone and took a cubed chunk of blubber, muktuk, between my fingers. It felt like the bottom of my canvas runners.

Reluctantly, I put it in my mouth. It was rubbery

Muktuk is made from the blubber and skin of a whale.
It is enjoyed by the Inuit as a rich source of vitamin C.

and strange to chew and the taste made a gag come into my throat. I swallowed it down. The fish, which I reminded myself was called pipsi, was salty and the Eskimo ice cream was so rich that I wanted to stick my head in the bay to wash away the taste. It all sat in my guts, filling me with a heavy, greasy feeling. I was hungry and I  wanted to please my mother, but it was too much.

It was all too much: the way my little brother studied me as if I were a strange species of fish that had washed ashore, and the way my mother touched the ends of my hair and sobbed that her little girl had been turned into an outsider. I no longer belonged to my own family.

I assured my mother that I wasn't an outsider—that I was still her daughter—"No, no... It's me, I'm still the same"—but my words came out in English, which she could not understand, instead of Inuvialuktun, our native tongue. She cried even harder.

This was not the reunion I had dreamed of for two years, every long Arctic summer day without darkness and every longer sunless winter night. I just wanted to go home. I wanted us to load up the *North Star* right that minute and travel back across the Arctic Ocean to Banks Island, where my family always spent most of the year. Everything would be fine once we returned home, where I would be sur- rounded only by our small community of friends, far from all the outsiders, except for those who traveled with us and practiced our ways and not the ways of the nuns. Banks Island was a million miles from the school in Aklavik, far enough that the outsiders would be unlikely to come for me again. I needed the open ground beneath my feet. I needed to look out across the land, dotted only by our tents. I needed to climb the hill above the cemetery and see a world that was truly our own. In that world, the outsiders' spell on me could be broken, and I could forget.

"When do we leave for Banks Island?" I asked my father, as I scanned the boats down the shore for my beloved *North Star*.

"Oh, Olemaun," he said to me in English, which he had learned at an outsiders' school many years ago, "we won't be going back. We have decided to stay here. We are going to try hunting and trading here in Tuk, and I can pick up extra work as a special constable for the RCMP. Mr. Carpenter will be leaving on the *North Star* without us."

I felt like a fish pulled up and flopped onto the ice—helpless and unable to find my way back to where I could breathe.

Instead of walking down the shoreline to our people's camp, next to the place where they had moored their schooners, we headed to the village. Over and over, I looked back at the bay. I was glad to be free of the brothers, but I had not left the outsiders' world. I still was not home, and now I knew that I would not even be going there.

RCMP: Royal Canadian Mounted Police. Canada's national police force.   15

schooner: a type of sailing vessel with masts.

See photo on page 111.

When we passed the Hudson's Bay Company store, my mother asked my father to stop and buy me some of the outsiders' food. He laughed for a good while and told her that I was still Inuvialuit: when I got hungry enough, I would eat. My mother and I looked at each other. Neither of us was sure.

My spirits lifted when we made it to our canvas tent, which was set up on a wooden frame near a small lake a short way past the village. My father's dogs greeted me with yelps and barks. We had no animals at the school and I had missed them so much. I reached out to pet one of the nine sled dogs, but it nearly took my hand off.

"Wait until you wear our scent again," my father said, drawing back the canvas door.

I followed him into the darkness, and stood blinking as my eyes adjusted. Then I smiled a slow smile. It was exactly as I remembered it, just as it had been on Banks Island. The cookstove stood near the center, the table close to it, and my mother and father's bed was against the south wall. I leaned forward, ready to race for the spot under their bed where I had always

See photo on page 112.

16

Hudson's Bay Company: the oldest surviving company in North America, incorporated by a royal charter in 1670. Hunters and trappers traded their pelts there for goods and supplies.

slept, but stopped myself. It probably belonged to one of my siblings now. I looked to my mother and she nodded with a smile. It was still mine! I dove under the big bed and onto the quilt that covered my small mattress. As I rolled to face the far side, I saw a small stack of my half-sister Rosie's books, which she must have left behind after her last visit. I was so excited to have something to read, but I was sorry I had missed seeing her. I wanted to tell her how bad I felt for not believing her when she warned me how awful the school was.

So many things had happened already and it was barely past lunch. I really needed to talk to someone like my big sister, who understood what I was going through, but I would have to settle for her books. I just wanted to curl up in my bed with them and drift off to sleep while the warm red glow of my father's pipe illuminated the dark tent.

My father peeked his head under the bed to see what I thought of the books. I hugged one to my chest. It was such a gift. My father had a kettle in his hand, and as he rose to put it on the stove I crawled out

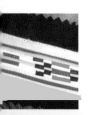

*Delta
Braid*

from my sleeping place, still hugging the book. My mother was at the foot of their bed, searching through the large wooden chest that held her things. At last, she pulled out one of her old parkas, a rich burgundy one embroidered with cream flowers. A detailed Delta braid ran around the hem. Lace decorated the shoulders and the wrists, and a stunning burst of wolf fur stood up around the hood. I remembered how beautiful she had looked in it long ago when we had come to a wedding here in Tuk. It was my favorite of her parkas. She looked at it a moment, then set it in my lap.

"For me?" I asked, pressing the fur to my face.

She smiled and nodded, understanding my gesture if not my words.

My sisters came through the door of the tent with my brother just as I pulled it over my head. I was now as big as my mother, and I felt very grown-up in her parka as I strutted around the tent for all my family to see. Elizabeth narrowed her eyes. I could tell she was envious, but I felt no pity. My mother's parka could not take away two years of shivering in my thin, ill-fitting uniform and canvas bloomers, nor could it make me

Delta braid, made by cutting pieces from long strips of fabric and layering them in a pattern, was used to decorate Mother Hubbard parkas.

forget the shame of be-
ing forced by a cruel nun
to wear the school's only
pair of bright red stock-
ings. Being teased about
how fat my legs looked
in them had been the
most humiliating expe-
rience of my life. But the
fur of the parka's hood
against my face helped
me to feel like I was no

longer that powerless girl. I needed my mother's parka
in a way my sisters could never understand.

   We drank tea and I did my best to answer my
family's questions, my father translating everything
at first. After a short time, a few of our words came
back to me, but I was not able to respond to many
of the questions on my own. It was frustrating. After
only two years away, I could barely speak my own
language. I had tried to preserve my memory of it, but
what I had retained was like a clump of dry dirt that

turned to dust in my hand. I wanted to laugh and giggle with my sisters, to tell them stories and teach them what I had learned, but my words were too few. I could speak to them only with a phrase or two and my heartfelt smiles.

"Mamaqtuq," I said, pointing to my tea—tastes good.

Everyone smiled, and my mother's smile was widest of them all.

My sisters pulled out two dolls that my father had made for them and begged me to play. I shook my head, because I had no doll of my own. At the school I had made a doll from scraps of fabric one of the sisters had given to me, but before I left I gave it to a smaller girl who was not going home.

My sisters pawed at me for attention. I had no words to tell them why I did not want to play their game. Mabel picked up a caribou-hide ball, and Elizabeth pulled me outside by the arm. We tossed the ball and ran until I forgot how homesick I was for Banks Island and how much I missed my friends from the school. It was so good to be back with my family.

By suppertime, I was very hungry, but still I could

not eat. My mother stared at the table and cried. She worried that I would starve to death, but my father said something to her, then turned to me and spoke in English. "You'll eat when you're ready, won't you?"

I was as unsure as my mother. The pain in my stomach was growing, and I wondered when my body would know that it was ready.

Before bed that first night, the family gathered around me as I read aloud from a book that a kind nun had given to me. Mabel was the same age I had been when I fell in love with the stories my big sister Rosie would read to me. Elizabeth was the same age I had been when my love for those stories and my desire to read them led me to the outsiders' school. I wished Rosie were there to watch our siblings listening as intently as I once had, even though they could not understand the words. My sisters' eyes grew wide in the dim light as they strained to comprehend what

I was telling them. My brother Ernest sat on my lap and looked at the pictures. My father translated for me, and they all marveled that I could now decipher the outsiders' words. Even my mother was impressed. I could tell by the way she kept looking up from her sewing.

Just as I was getting to a good part, my father looked up from his seat at the table and told us it was time to go to sleep. My mother tucked my sisters into the bed they shared and my brother got under the covers of my mother and father's bed. I crawled under the warm blankets beneath where my parents slept and gazed out at the glow of embers from my father's pipe. A heavy, ocean-like sleep settled over me and I drifted off to the dream time.

It wasn't Banks Island, but it *was* home. Even though I missed my friends at the school, nothing would ever make me go back. I belonged here in this tent with my family. I wasn't able to hide away on a distant island, but maybe, just maybe, the dark walls would ward off the outsiders' spell.

Chapter TWO

I WOKE LONG BEFORE everyone else.

At the school the nuns got everyone out of bed at five o'clock, winter and summer, to do the endless chores they required of us. We mopped floors, we scrubbed walls, we emptied the buckets of waste from the latrine, we hauled cords of firewood and stacked them into mountains.

See photo on page 112.

I crawled out from under my parents' bed and sat at the kitchen table. What was I to do with myself while everyone slept? It seemed odd to wake to silence:

no screaming nuns, no groaning girls. Only the quiet breaths of my sleeping family.

And the growl of my stomach. Hunger was nothing new to me, but all I had eaten since breakfast the day before was a small sample of my mother's food. I had to eat something.

There was also a chill in the tent, so I prepared the cook fire, thinking about what I might be able to make that I could stomach. I knew my parents would have the ingredients for bannock. I had watched them both make it many times. I remembered loving bannock, warm and fresh from the oven and covered with lard. It was just another type of bread, and bread was the only thing I truly liked eating at the school. I was sure I could figure out how to mix it.

I got a bowl out of one of the chests where we kept our things and set it on the table. Then I rummaged through the supplies until I found a canister of flour. I dumped some into the bowl and added a heap of baking soda. Next I poured in a cup of salt and a couple of tablespoons of sugar. I stirred in a little water and some fat, and started kneading the

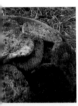

Bannock

24

Bannock, often referred to as frybread, is a common food staple of Aboriginal peoples in North America. Flour, water, and baking powder are mixed into a dough, which is then shaped into a circle and baked or fried, sometimes over an open fire.

dough. I wanted to be certain that it was mixed well, so I kneaded for a long time. When I was done, I pressed the heavy dough flat into a pan, opened the cast iron door of the cookstove, and slid it into the cooking chamber.

I knew it would take a while to bake, but I kept looking in the cookstove anyway. Nothing seemed to be happening. I took out a book of children's Bible stories and sat at the table to read just one page while I waited.

"What is burning?" my father said, raising himself on one arm.

I slammed the book shut and jumped to my feet. How much time had passed? I couldn't be sure. I hadn't meant to get so carried away, but one page had led to another and another. Now my breakfast was burning. I leaped to grab it out of the stove, but I burned the tip of my finger and had to pull my hand back. I had forgotten to use a rag to grasp the handle.

"What on earth are you doing?" my father asked me.

"I'm making bannock," I told him.

He crawled out of bed and pulled on his parka.

"Well, let's see," he said. He pulled the pan from the stove with a thick piece of cloth and lifted out the blackened disc. He tried sinking his teeth into it without much luck. A smile crossed his face. "Olemaun, that isn't bannock. It's ban-brick. How long did you knead it?"

"I worked the dough for a really long time so it would be well mixed," I said.

"Ah, that pushes all the air out." He tilted his head. "What did you put in it?"

I pointed to the ingredients, which still sat on the table. He picked up the baking soda and started to laugh. "Baking soda? That would be why it tastes so bad. You're supposed to use baking powder." He held out the bannock, examining it and clucking his tongue against the roof of his mouth to lose the taste. "How much salt did you use?"

"This much," I said showing him with my hands and trying to hold back the tears.

My father walked to the door of the tent and I followed him. I watched as he tossed the bannock out the door. It bounced on the ground and landed at the feet of one of his sled dogs. The dog took one sniff,

whimpered, and ran away from it. I wanted to laugh, but a tear fell down my face. My father brushed it away with his thumb. "Come," he said. "I'll make you breakfast."

My father made the best sourdough pancakes in the world. I wanted to ask that we pray before we ate, but I was so happy to be sharing that moment with him. I had not forgotten what the nuns told me, though: it was my responsibility to save the souls of my family from Hell. I promised myself to bring it up as soon as the time seemed right.

My mother was angry when she woke. Supplies were expensive and she complained about the flour and salt I had wasted.

"She was hungry," my father said. He looked at me. "And it won't happen again, will it?" he added in English.

I shook my head. My mother relented, and she and my siblings joined us at the table.

After we finished the pancakes my father told us to get ready. The supply barge, which came only twice a year—once in the spring and once in late summer— was expected today. With supplies from the barge, the Carpenters, the Wolkis, and the rest of our friends would be leaving for Banks Island. It hit me as though someone had just splashed cold Arctic seawater in my face. We really *weren't* going home.

"Cheer up," my father told me. "At least here in Tuk

you'll be close to Agnes. You can play with her when-
ever you choose."

Agnes and I had known each other all our lives,
but when her mother started to get sick they had left
Banks Island and moved to Tuk. I met up with Agnes
again at the school, where she was my best friend. The
thought of seeing her every day cheered me a little.

I put on my new parka, pulled some beautiful
kamik onto my feet (they had also belonged to my
mother), and trailed after my family out of the tent.

Kamik

I studied the square wooden buildings as we
walked down the bare dirt main street of Tuktoyaktuk.
Some canvas tents lined the street, as on Banks Island,
but quickly they gave way to log cabins and other
wooden buildings. Despite my happiness at home
with my family, I still felt that I needed to get away
from buildings and places where so many people
lived so close together. This was still the outsiders'
world. I didn't want to be here; I wanted to be board-
ing the *North Star* and setting out across the Arctic
Ocean to Banks Island, to where I was raised.

By the time we reached the shore, my feet were

*Kamik are a type of soft boot worn by
the Inuit. They are also called mukluks.*

*See photo
on page 113.*

sore from the soft-soled kamik, and our friends had already packed their tents and possessions onto their schooners, which were lined up along the shore.

I had to look away. The scene was more than I could bear.

In the distance, the massive barge appeared, a stern-wheeler pushing it down the river and across the bay toward the bank. I wanted to cheer like everyone else, but I didn't.

Aboard the barge would be drums of fuel, fresh fruit, new dresses from Eaton's, hunting rifles, mail, and even secret government crates. When the barge docked, everyone would rush toward it, eager to see the goodies aboard. Among the crowd milling around on the riverbank were women waiting for new cooking pots and boys waiting for their first rifle. The anticipation was high. The arrival of the supply barge was like Christmas in the North, but this time for me its coming was bittersweet. Once the supplies were loaded, the schooners would leave for Banks Island without us.

My mother and father talked with the other adults to pass the time. I saw Agnes through the crowd,

Eaton's: The T. Eaton Co. Limited was once Canada's largest department store. Their mail order catalogues allowed people in rural communities to buy many things that would have been unavailable to them otherwise.

holding on to her mother's arm. I fought my way on to her side and smiled at her. There was so much I wanted to talk to her about.

"Hello," I said, my smile turning to a grin. "Don't you wish we were leaving on those boats too?"

She turned away from her mother and smiled back at me, but just as she opened her mouth, her mother yanked on her arm and hissed into her ear. I could hear the words, and they were simple enough that I understood.

"No English," Agnes's mother said.

The smile vanished from Agnes's face. She turned away from her mother as if she would stand her ground, as if she would speak to me even though her mother had forbidden it. But sick though her mother was, she seemed to be pretty strong. She yanked her daughter away into the crowd, and I struggled not to weep.

After a moment, I walked away from the crowd and sat on a rock, watching from afar. My sisters and their playmates amused themselves with their homemade dolls, but no one said anything to me. Perhaps I had been gone for so long they no longer knew who I was. I waited for the children I had once played with to remember me. They didn't. They had all grown in the past two years, but they still looked the same. Everything about me must have seemed so different to them. I had spent some time that morning gazing into Mother's one small mirror, taking in my short hair and hollow cheeks, my lean body and my hardened eyes. I *was* different.

As she turned to board a schooner, one of the women ruffled my brother's hair with her hand. The way that everyone touched and the kind manner in which they spoke to each other, expressing sorrow at saying good-bye and happiness for years of shared memories, overwhelmed me and filled me with yearning all at the same time.

As I watched, the barge and its paddle wheeler came to a standstill against the shore, and the captain appeared on deck. I expected everyone to surge forward and eagerly start unpacking the barge, but as I turned my attention from the boat to the crowd I saw that the majority of the people were now looking back toward the mainland.

I had to squeeze between a few people to get a look, and I could not have anticipated the sight that met my eyes. Making his way toward the Hudson's Bay store was a dark man who moved liked a grizzly on its hind feet. His hair sprang from his head in tight, kinky spirals like a strange dark moss, unlike that of the black men I had seen in books, who wore their hair very short. He also had bundles of pelts slung over his shoulder and tied around his waist by a belt.

I had heard the elders talk in hushed tones about this man, but to me he had always been an abstract idea, like a spirit. To see him now was shocking. My chest tightened.

As he neared, the crowd took a step backward toward the shore, and I felt them collectively holding their breath. But the man just continued on to the store. My mother pulled me back to the rear of the crowd. "Du-bil-ak," she whispered to me and my siblings... the devil.

A mosquito-like buzz arose from the men in the crowd as they turned back to begin unloading the barge. I couldn't wait to see what was on board.

I looked around for the dark stranger who had just shown up, but he could no longer be seen.

When my mother also noticed that he was gone, she took my sisters tightly by the hand and led us back to our tent, not allowing us to stay and help with the unloading. Elizabeth strained to catch sight of the dark stranger as my mother cut a wide berth around the store. I was curious too, though much less so than she was. He was quite a spectacle, his massive frame towering over the heads of the people in the crowd, but I just wanted him to go away. His arrival had cheated me out of the one day a year that was bigger than Christmas, and out of saying good-bye to our friends.

See photo on page 113.

EVERYONE EXPECTED THAT once the dark stranger my mother called the Du-bil-ak had sold his pelts and collected his supplies, he would go away to wherever it was that he came from. Until then, I had to stay close to home. I was not even allowed to go find Agnes. I couldn't believe how unreasonable my mother was being. Agnes was my best friend in all the world. My only friend.

I longed to talk with someone who would not look at me with disappointment every time I stumbled to find the Inuvialuktun word I needed, or each time confusion overtook me because I could not understand what was being said. I wanted to ask Agnes if she could eat the food of our people. I wanted to know what she thought of the giant. Instead, I was stuck with my little sisters pestering me while I tried to lose myself in a book, trying to forget that we were not aboard the *North Star* on our way home.

Chapter THREE

I N THE AFTERNOON, my mother came to find
me to go fishing with her. I resented that my
sisters were allowed to tag along. I wanted to have
my mother to myself and tried to ask if we might go
alone. I pulled at her sleeve and pointed out the door,
then pointed from my sisters to their bed. She shook
her head. Spit flew from her mouth as she talked
about the Du-bil-ak and pointed toward the village. I
guessed that she was scared to leave the girls at home
alone. My father had bundled Ernest up in the sled

and taken him along on his search for wood, and I
was sorry he hadn't taken Mabel and Elizabeth too.

We walked to the lake near our home, called
Felix Lake. We found a spot on the far shore and my
mother and sisters dropped their lines into the water.
I just stood there, growing increasingly conscious
of the glances from my sisters, who had noticed that
I had yet to drop my own line in the lake. What if I
had forgotten how to fish? What would they think of
me? My mother nudged me to go ahead; I could stall
no longer. I took a deep breath and followed suit, and
they lost interest in me.

My mother was an excellent fisherwoman, and she hauled in one lake trout and then another. She caught more than my sisters and I combined. Normally I was a very competitive person and would have tried to outdo her, but my spirits were low.

My mother noticed I was acting strangely and asked me what was wrong. I understood her question but could find no words to answer her with, to explain what I was feeling. I shrugged my shoulders and shook my head. She looked unconvinced, so I jerked at my fishing line and pretended to have a nibble. Just as my mother was about to help me, Mabel squealed with delight. She had caught a fish, and I could tell it was of a fair size by the way she struggled with it. My mother turned to help her. The fish was a ten-pound lake trout. Mabel grinned from ear to ear, holding up the flailing fish for us to see. My mother patted her on the back while Elizabeth oohed and aahed. It *was* a big fish, but I didn't think it warranted all that fanfare.

My sisters giggled and chattered, gesturing with their arms, and my mother tossed her head back and laughed. They were recalling other fishing trips, other fish they had caught together; I was not a part of any of it. I could not even join in their conversation. I wanted my family to be proud of a fish I had caught. I dropped my hook back into the water and prayed I would catch a fish even bigger than Mabel's.

We caught more than enough fish that afternoon, though Mabel still outdid me.

Sik-sik

As we walked back toward our tent, I trailed behind with my mother while my sisters ran ahead after a small sik-sik that had bravely popped its head up out of the tundra. A pair of ducks scattered into the air before them, and Mabel and Elizabeth fell to their knees, searching for eggs in the grass. My mother prodded me gently, so I handed her my string of fish and ran to join my sisters. We found four eggs, one for each of us children to have for supper along with the fish. At least I wasn't going to starve. Between bannock, fish, and eggs, I could survive.

See photo on page 114.

My father was waiting for us at the site of our new home. His face was red and sweaty from work. He was carving logs he had found adrift in the ocean, so that they would fit together into walls.

Sik-sik is the Inuit name for the Arctic ground squirrel, which is also referred to as a gopher.

"Igloo," explained Elizabeth, using the Inuktitut word for house and pointing to my father.

My brother played on the ground with a heap of small pieces of driftwood, pretending to build his own little house.

My father had been raised by his grandfather in a log home. I knew that he had always wanted to build us one, but our nomadic lives had not been suited to it. Now that we were staying in Tuk, he could finally build a log cabin for us. Everyone else was excited about the house, but to me it was just one more thing that meant we weren't going back to Banks Island.

After the fish were cleaned and cooked, my father came in to wash up for supper. As everyone began to eat, I decided it was time I brought up something that was bothering me greatly.

"You didn't say grace," I said to Father.

"We don't say grace in this house," he replied, reaching for a piece of fish.

"But you have to. I think we should read from the Bible too. Don't you want your soul to be saved?"

He glared at me and brought a fist down on the

Inuktitut: the name commonly used to refer collectively to the different dialects spoken by Inuit peoples across the far north of Canada and Alaska and one of the official languages of both Nunavut and the Northwest Territories.

table. "I *have* read the Bible. It was the only book I had when I left residential school, and I read it twice during my first year back out on the trapline. Just stories. That's all I found in it, so you can leave that God business at the school. I do not want to hear about it before I eat."

"But the nuns and the priests said you are going to Hell. You are all going to Hell, because you don't know God!" I cried. "I don't want you to go to Hell!"

My father ignored my pleas. He grabbed the platter of fish from the center of the table and heaped some onto his plate. My sisters look relieved, but I felt ill. My father had read the Bible. How could he not know better? Why would he want his family to spend eternity in damnation? And what of my little sisters and my brother? I said grace silently in my head six times, once for each of them and once for Olemaun, because Margaret knew about kneeling and bowing and praying, but Olemaun did not. I felt like a bad Christian and a bad daughter for not trying harder to convert them. I decided I would read my sisters one of the stories from my children's Bible before bed to make up for it.

Despite my misery over the fate of my family's souls, I devoured an entire fish and my egg. My mother and father couldn't believe how much I ate. The pancakes I had eaten earlier that day had been far from enough to tide me over.

Later I was sorry that I hadn't eaten a second fish. For the next two days, I was not offered a thing that I could stomach. They were trying to force me to eat the foods I used to. It didn't seem fair. Olemaun couldn't eat cabbage soup and Margaret couldn't eat pipsi. Over and over, I tucked my head into a book and let my imagination release my hunger pains.

See photo on page 116.

ON MY FIFTH MORNING at home, I sat at the table where my father liked to read, engrossed in one of my books and trying not to think of the breakfast I had not touched. The book was called *Gulliver's Travels* and told the story of a man who traveled to faraway lands. One of the lands was filled with strange little people called Lilliputians, who imprisoned Gulliver— to them, he was a giant. I wondered if the Du-bil-ak,

44

as my mother called him, felt like Gulliver among us. I also wondered what the little people would have done to me, if I had been stranded on their shores.

I jumped when my mother placed a cup of tea in front of me. She gestured to the door of our tent, meaning that I should take it out to my father. I stood up too quickly, and the world tightened into a narrow tunnel and went black. When I awoke, my mother was standing over me, staring down. I rose to my feet as quickly as I was able, still feeling light-headed. My mother grabbed me by the arm and marched me out the door. My father asked her where she was taking me, but she did not answer. She was not going to argue with him about it.

I was thankful when I realized that we were headed to the Hudson's Bay Company, though I felt so weak I wasn't sure I could make it. Her decision came just in time. I was almost ready to give in and eat the strong-smelling, salty food that my family somehow enjoyed.

See photo on page 114.

My mother took me with her because she could not read and did not trust the clerk at the store. We walked up the steps of the white-painted wooden cabin and through the door. As we made our way to the counter, my mother still had a firm grip on my arm to steady me. She looked to me to point out what I wanted. I shrugged my shoulders. I hated the outsiders' food almost as much as our own. She let out an impatient breath and began pointing to tins and cans on the shelf behind the man at the counter, picking out things like corned beef and canned beans. They were not the sorts of things they had fed at us at the school, and I was not sure I would have more luck eating them, but I had to get something into my stomach. My mother was not about to make the rest of the family live on bannock and fish on my account. I understood that, though I knew the outsiders' food was also not the answer.

Just as she was pointing to some tinned peaches, something I could definitely eat, a deep, throaty cough startled us. The store was not well lit and our eyes had not fully adjusted from the glaring sun; we had not noticed anyone else in the store, besides the clerk. We turned toward the sound, which came from the back of the store.

"Du-bil-ak," whispered my mother, when she saw
the large, dark-skinned man standing in front of
the bookcase. I could not take my eyes off the dark
stranger as he fingered the books in the case, even as
my mother dragged me toward the door, keeping us
as far away from him as possible.

My mother nearly ran down the stairs of the build-
ing, her breath short and quick with terror. Why was
the grizzly-like outsider still here? He should have

sold his pelts, gathered his supplies, and moved on days before. Now I would have to eat the same food as my family or starve. No peaches.

Defeated, I struggled to keep up with my mother, my feet sore from wearing my kamik. When we arrived home I went inside the tent and gorged myself on muktuk, until I could not stuff in another rubbery bite.

"See? I told you, when she was hungry enough, she would eat," my father said to my mother in Inuvial-uktun on his way out the door to find out what was going on with the dark stranger. Somehow, I understood every word.

Chapter FOUR

WHEN I WOKE THE NEXT morning, I resolved to visit my friend Agnes. Except for the previous summer, when she was with her mother, we had not spent a day apart in two years. Now, between her mother's rejection of me and my own mother's fear of the Du-bil-ak, it seemed as if we would never see each other again. After breakfast, I followed my father outside and stood quietly while he prepared his tools to chisel the logs.

"What is on your mind?" he asked me, seeing the determination on my face.

"I would like to go play with Agnes today," I told him.

"Your mother wants you close to home, with the stranger around."

"Do you think he is the devil?" I asked.

"No," my father laughed, "I don't think he's the devil."

"Where did he come from?"

"I'm not sure. Some people say he traveled here with one of the Klinkenbergs who stole a boat from the States, and others say he was a whaler but was left behind. I don't think anyone really knows."

"Why is he still here?"

"I don't know. Maybe there was trouble back where he came from."

"No, why is he still in Tuk?" I asked. "If he has his supplies, why doesn't he leave town, now that he has what he needs?"

"Maybe loneliness. When you spend a lot of time out hunting and checking the traplines by yourself, it can be very lonely. I imagine he just wants to be around people for a while."

"So he's here to be around us, even though no one wants him here?" I said.

"Yeah," my father replied, dropping his eyes to the ground. "Even though no one wants him here. I'm guessing he'll be gone soon. Don't worry, Olemaun."

"What if he never leaves? Will I have to go back to the school to be able to play with Agnes?"

"No, but aren't you scared to walk in town with that man around?"

I shook my head. "Not really. I saw a picture of Lena Horne when I was at the outsiders' school, and she is dark like that."

See photo on page 115.

My father had a collection of Lena Horne's albums that he played on a hand-cranked record player. She was his favorite singer. He looked amused, and I could tell he hadn't known that she had dark skin like the trapper.

"I promise to be very careful," I assured him.

"Go on," he told me. "I will tell your mother."

I kissed my father and ran toward town. Agnes would be so excited. We could go hunting for eggs. She was probably having the same problems eating that I was.

I was almost out of breath by the time I reached

her door. I pounded on it with my fist and waited for an answer. I couldn't wait to see Agnes's face when she saw me standing there. After what seemed like ages, the door opened. Her mother was on the other side, with a very stern look on her pale face. She had always been friendly to me on Banks Island, but today she seemed angry. She turned and gestured over her shoulder, and Agnes appeared at her side.

But when I stepped in to talk to my friend, she moved back timidly and turned to her mother. Then she turned back to me.

"Would you like to go hunting for eggs?" I asked.

She stared at the toes of her kamik. "I am not allowed."

I stared at her, trying to determine why her mother would not allow her to come with me. "If it's because of the dark stranger," I said at last, "we can play here. We don't have to go out."

"It's not because of the stranger," she said. "It's because of you."

Her words took the breath out of me. I groped to say something, but my thoughts and emotions were fast runners that I could not tame with words.

"My mother and father say I am an outsider now," she whispered, glancing over her shoulder at her mother as she spoke the English words. "They do not want me playing with children like you—children from the school. They don't want me speaking English, or praying, or doing anything like a white person."

Agnes had gone to the school for much longer than I had, because her mother hadn't been able to care for her. Yet I remembered Agnes speaking Inuvialuktun on rare occasions at the school, though it was forbidden. Agnes once confessed to me that she secretly gave the objects around her their Inuvialuktun names and that sometimes she would practice conversations in her head in our native tongue. Because of this she had not forgotten how to speak the language. Whereas I had been so eager to learn the new ways, I had not thought to hold on to the old ones.

Her mother spoke to her in a stern tone and I strained to figure out the meaning of her words.

"I'm sorry," Agnes said, giving me a half-smile and blinking back tears as she closed the door.

I walked down to the point. It was the closest I could get to Banks Island without a boat. I didn't want to go back to the tent, where I only disappointed my mother and could barely speak with my sisters. I didn't want to tell my father that his daughter was not good enough to play with her own best friend. My tears fell into the ocean, and I wished my spirit was in those tears, because then I could follow the current back to a place where I belonged.

Gradually I became aware that I was not alone. Standing twenty feet behind me was the Du-bil-ak. I wanted to turn and run, but what if he ran after me? I stood my ground, trying to decide what to do, and then realized that he hadn't even noticed I was there. His eyes were fixed on the horizon, as mine had been. I knew I should try to sneak away, but curiosity held me to the spot. His massive shoulders were slumped forward and his entire body breathed longing. I wiped my tears on the sleeve of my parka and straightened. He didn't look so much like a devil at this distance. Some of the nuns at the school in Aklavik looked far scarier than he did, and in his expression I saw something I recognized: homesickness.

In that moment, he turned to look at me. I sucked in a quick, startled breath and stood frozen in my kamik. He looked at me and the corners of his mouth flinched as though he wanted to smile, but had forgotten how to do it.

Then he turned away and set off toward the village.

Chapter FIVE

I HAD A FITFUL SLEEP that night. It was the same bad dream over and over again, every time I closed my eyes. I dreamed that I was back at the outsiders' school, locked inside the skirt of one of the nuns' habits. The nun told me that she would let me out if I could remember my name and if my mother could recognize me. My parents and the others from the village had become very small. They pointed through the bars and laughed. Agnes knew where the key was to free me, but in the distance I could see her aboard the *North Star,* sailing away to Banks Island without me.

It was late when my mother finally woke me; my sisters had already run off to play with their friends. My mother was tired of hearing them complain about being cooped up and had finally decided that there was no harm in letting them run loose. Above me, my brother was playing with a ball on my parents' bed. I kneeled and began to say my prayers. My mother pulled me to my feet. I backed away from her, fighting down fury. How could she stop me from doing something so important? How could she condemn me to damnation along with the rest of my family?

See photo on page 115.

But she seemed oblivious to my anger. The look on her face was eager, childlike. In her hand she held the book I had been reading. She tugged me by the arm, nodding for me to come. My prayers would have to wait.

I joined her at the table, where a cold piece of bannock was waiting for me. I fell upon it, ravenous.

My mother set the book in front of us and pointed at it. "Read," she said in Inuvialuktun.

I swallowed the bannock in my mouth. *"Gulliver's Travels,"* I said out loud.

"No," she said in English, shaking her head. And then she repeated the word "read." I wasn't sure what she wanted of me, so I opened the book and began reading aloud.

"No," she said again and pointed from the page to herself. "Me."

My mother wanted me to teach her to read, but it wasn't as simple as opening the book and doing it. She didn't even know how to speak English. How could she expect to read it?

I thought for a moment while I chewed and swallowed another bite. Maybe if I taught her to write her name she would be satisfied. I found a small scrap of paper and a pencil and printed her name, which happened to be the same as that of my father's favorite singer: *Lena*. Then I handed the paper to her and

Ulu Knife

pointed for her to write below it. She shook her head like a shy student. I handed her the pencil and smiled to reassure her.

The pencil was awkward in her hand. First she held it in her palm as if it were a rocker-like ulu knife, but she soon realized she could not write like that. Then she tried holding it as she would a sewing needle. She was very skilled with both of those instruments, but no one had ever taught her how to hold a pencil. She fumbled with it, and it fell to the floor. I picked it up and gave it to her again. She took it reluctantly, grasping it in her palm. I pulled it out of her hand and slipped it between her pointer and middle fingers and helped her to draw the first letter. Her expression brightened. I let go of her hand so that she could do it herself. She pressed too hard. The lead broke and the pencil went flying. I rose to retrieve it, but she crumpled and tore the paper in her hands and threw it down. I was silent. Why couldn't she ask my father to teach her? He could explain to her in Inuvialuktun what she needed to do.

I didn't want my mother to think I didn't believe

The ulu, a knife with a rocker-like blade, is traditionally used by Inuit women for tasks such as scraping hides, cutting hair, or preparing food.

she was smart enough to learn. But she tossed Rosie's book at me angrily. I had no way to tell her why I wasn't giving her the magic secret it would take to read the book. When I didn't say anything, she yelled at me.

I shut my ears to her until the world was silent, then pulled my kamik onto my tender feet.

I ran toward town, cut down the bank at the Hudson's Bay Company, and ran along the shore, faster and faster. I had strong legs and loved to run, especially there, where I could feel the salt in my lungs. I was in full stride when a stone dropped me, and I fell, skinning my knees. I rolled over and pulled the kamik off my throbbing foot. The pad near my big toe was already bruised and swollen. I had spent two years cursing the outsiders' shoes and longing for the footwear of my people. Now that I had them, every pebble pierced the soft skin of my feet.

The pain made me angry, and that gave me energy, so I stood up and ran again, ignoring the stinging in my knees and foot. I didn't stop until I reached a large tide pool. I found a place to sit and I sank my throbbing, swollen foot into the cold water. Soon it felt numb.

When I had caught my breath again, I realized I couldn't run anymore, so I hobbled back toward the Hudson's Bay store, moving no faster than the wisp of cloud above me. I was in no hurry to go home.

Children played in front of one of the houses, but I pretended not to see them. A woman came out of her cabin and stopped me. She was friendly and chattered away. I knew her from Banks Island. She had wintered there, like my family, until her husband died. She was very old, an elder, and I didn't want to show her disrespect. She waited for my answers, at first with anticipation, and then with annoyance, but I had no idea what she was saying. All I could reply was, "Sorry."

Disgusted by my rudeness, she threw her hands into the air and walked back to her cabin, shaking her head and muttering to herself. My mother was already angry enough. When she heard about this, I was sure to be in trouble. Not only had I disrespected an elder, but I had also made it public that I was like an outsider now.

I was afraid of everyone I passed the rest of the way. I was fearful that my own people would try to talk to me and be angry when I couldn't answer, and I was even more fearful of the two English-speaking missionaries I saw standing outside the small log-cabin church. I was scared that they would take me into that dark church and make me kneel and pray to make up for being a bad daughter—for doing something to embarrass my parents, and more importantly for not convincing them to say grace. I never wanted to see or speak to another person again.

I breathed a huge sigh of relief when I caught sight of our tent. I greeted my mother and father stoically, holding back the sadness that filled my heart, and disappeared inside. I pulled off my kamik and rubbed my raw and bruised feet between my hands. Then I did something I never could have predicted. I took my school stockings out from under my parents' bed where I had stowed them. I put on the thick gray wool tights and slipped my feet into my canvas runners. The first time I had put my feet in outsiders' shoes they had pinched and felt hard and awkward. Now they were a barrier, protection against the hard earth.

I left the tent more comfortably than I had entered it, though even in the runners my feet ached. I did not say a word to my parents. Once again, I didn't have the Inuvialuktun words to explain myself to them. I stood beside my father and waited for him to give me a job to do.

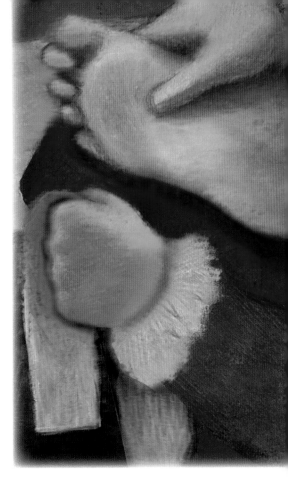

Chapter SIX

I HUNG MY HEAD AT SUPPER and prayed for
God to save the souls of my parents and my
siblings. Elizabeth said something. I looked up from
my prayers to find everyone at the table staring at
me. My sister's face said that I was alien and weird.
Mabel wore the same expression. Then my father
pounded his work-worn hand on the tabletop and
we all jumped. No one spoke during dinner and I
had trouble finishing mine. After an hour, my mother
excused me from the table and sent me out to feed
the rest of my meal to the sled dogs.

I dumped the food in front of them and they lunged at it. The meal that I could not finish in an hour was consumed by the dogs in seconds.

I passed by my father on my way back into the tent. He looked up at me but did not speak, returning instead to marking the logs with a rock to show where he wanted to notch each one to fit with the others. His actions gave me an idea.

THE NEXT DAY I WALKED with my mother to the store to help her bring home some supplies. The same group of children I had seen the day before was playing a game with a caribou-hide ball outside. My mother indicated that I should stay and play with them. I stood on the step and crossed my arms. I didn't know how to ask to join them, and I was pretty sure they wouldn't welcome me.

The girl who was holding the ball stopped and walked my way. She was at least three years younger than I was, as were the rest of the children, who followed. She leaned in close to me and asked me a question. I wasn't sure what she was saying. All I could say was, "Sorry." She gave me a hard but curious look.

A boy stepped in closer and said something to me. Again I responded with, "Sorry," shaking my head in apology.

Soon all the children were chattering around me like a flock of crows. My chest felt tight. I shook my head faster, repeating the only thing I knew to say.

They repeated it back to me in a taunt: "Sorry, sorry, sorry." From my place on the steps, I looked down my nose at them like Gulliver staring down a crowd of Lilliputians, and stomped my good foot. They had some nerve to be so rude to me. I was much older than they were, after all.

The children pointed at my shoes and laughed. I turned from them and darted into the refuge of the store. My mother was at the counter, arguing with the clerk about a price. My mother was a small woman, but when she saw that I was behind her, she heaved up a large bag of flour and shoved it into my chest. I propped it over my shoulder. Her steps were heavy as she made her way across the room.

As we emerged into the blinding glare of the sun, the children began taunting me again. "Sorry, sorry, sorry," they sang, pointing at my shoes.

My mother looked to my feet, then back to the children. She clutched me by the arm with a hiss, which sent the children scurrying. I had embarrassed her, I knew it, but her free hand clung tight to me and she held her head high the whole way through town. As we passed one of the buildings, I saw the Du-bil-ak watching us from the shadows. Aside from my shoes, I may have looked like a normal Inuvialuit girl, but I was almost as strange to the people as he was. All of us who had been to the school were regarded as strange creatures, changed by our time away. Maybe my mother secretly thought that the outsiders had turned me into a du-bil-ak too.

When we got home, she took the bag of flour from me, threw it down, and began arguing with my father. I wasn't sure if it was about the clerk at the store or about me. I guessed it was probably me. Unnoticed, I walked away, straight toward the bay. I wasn't going anywhere near town ever again, and thankfully I didn't need to in order to carry out my secret plan to help my mother.

I selected a couple of large, flat stones and found a comfortable place to sit. With a chalk stone I wrote my mother's name on the first, with dotted lines that she could trace over and over without wasting paper. Paper was expensive and not always easy to get. On the second I drew the letters of the alphabet in the same way, just as the nuns had shown us. I knew my mother could learn this way. Now I had to make *her* believe it, too.

I gathered the stones, searched for a feather, and headed back to our tent. My mother was inside, putting my brother down for a nap.

"Here," I said, laying the stones on the table.

She came over to see. I showed her where I had written her name in dots. I took the feather and held it in my hand, tracing the letters to show her how she could use the dots to learn. I thought she would be very pleased, but she tossed the stones into a corner and began setting the table for supper. When we sat to eat, I did not see them in the corner anymore.

AFTER DOING THE DISHES, I went out to the dogs. When I first returned from school, I smelled foreign and they bared their teeth at me anytime I neared them. But now that I had been home more than a week and had regained the scent of my family, they greeted me with lapping kisses. All nine of my father's dogs vied to tumble and rub against me. I sank my

fingers deep into their warm fur and felt for their soft skin. Their fur was tickly, which made me laugh, as did their expressive eyes. I rolled around on the ground and giggled until I could no longer breathe. When I looked up, I saw that my father was watching me with joy spread across his face. He joined me on the ground and wrapped his arms around me.

"I'm sorry," he said, "for sending you to the school."

I was sorry, too. I should have listened to him when he told me not to go.

I THOUGHT MANY HOURS about the dark stranger no one spoke to. I wondered if he stayed near Tuk because it was easier to be rejected here than at home. Maybe he knew that if he returned to where he was from, he would be like an animal that carried a foreign scent, like I had when I came back from school. Maybe he didn't want his pack to reject him. It would have to be a strong fear like that to keep him away. He was completely alone here, apart from the Hudson's Bay clerk, who was rumored to play chess with him out of sight in the back of the store.

I passed the weeks that followed in solitude or playing with the dogs. Often I would read, working my way through the whole stack of books that had been so kindly left for me. Books were friends that held my hand through entire journeys. I read *Gulliver's*

See photo on page 116.

Travels twice, each time understanding more how Gulliver felt upon his return home.

It occurred to me that the Du-bil-ak was like Gulliver, and after my second reading of his travels I decided that the dark stranger needed the book more than I did. I walked down to the store to leave it with the clerk for him.

I entered the store, and standing at the counter was Agnes, who was fetching some supplies. When I came up beside her, she looked around to make sure that none of the elders were present, then threw her arms around me and hugged me tightly. "I missed you," she said in English.

As much as I had missed her too, I didn't say so. I knew it was not Agnes's fault that she couldn't see me, but I felt betrayed by her—abandoned.

"How is your mother?" I asked.

Agnes frowned. "She's getting worse."

"Oh. I am sorry to hear that."

"How are things with your family?" she asked me.

I shrugged my shoulders. I wanted to say that my family had missed me so much and they were so happy to have me back home. I wanted to say that it was just like I had never gone away. But that wasn't true, and Agnes would know it.

"At least we are home," she said in a quiet voice, and hugged me again. But we weren't home. Banks Island was home. I didn't know what to say, so I said nothing.

When we pulled apart, she noticed the book I had in my hand. "What do you have there?" she said.

I tried to hold back the burning in my cheeks, but I was caught. "Oh," I replied, "it's just a book I finished."

The sadness lifted from her eyes. "Which one?"

"*Gulliver's Travels.*"

She pulled it from my hand. "I've never read that one. I miss reading. We don't have any books. Do you think I could borrow it?" I watched, unsure what to do as she thumbed through the pages with so much enthusiasm. "I don't think my mother minds if I read in English. She doesn't like to hear me speak it, but she can't hear me read, can she? Do you mind?"

How could I object? "No, not at all," I said.

"Well, I better get back. My mother probably needs me." She signed for her goods and left the store, calling

"Quyannanini"—thank you—over her shoulder.

"Well, what do you want?" the clerk grumbled at me.

I gave him my best mean face and left the store myself. Agnes was walking ahead of me. I was glad I had shared the book with her, but I still wished I could give it to the Du-bil-ak. I should have just told her why I had brought the book to the Hudson's Bay store. I had other books I could have lent to her.

I was angry with myself the whole way home. We were both much better off than he was. We were at least Inuvialuit, and we had our families. It was not easy for Agnes to care for her mother, but she enjoyed being home from the school. And I had only to remember how to be Olemaun Pokiak, an Inuvialuit girl. Whereas the Du-bil-ak was not one of us at all. He was not even like the outsiders we were used to. Nothing he did would bring him family or friends.

IN LATE AUGUST, the Du-bil-ak walked away from town and did not return. Wherever he had gone, I hoped he would be able to find some peace. I was sad that he left before Agnes returned the book, but

I was glad she was enjoying it so much. It would give us something to talk about as soon as her mother was feeling well again and I could prove that my Inuvial-uktun was good enough for me to play with her.

See photo on page 117.

ON THE DAY THE OUTSIDERS' boat came back to gather up children, I hid under my parents' bed. My father had promised not to let them take me back to the school, but I was taking no chances. Agnes wasn't taking any chances either. Because her mother had taken a steep turn for the worse, it had been decided that Agnes should go back to the school and her mother back to the hospital. But when the boat came, no one could find her.

For two days the men from Tuk searched for Agnes. When she couldn't be found, speculation spread about what had happened to her. Some people thought that maybe she'd been eaten by a polar bear, while others said that the Du-bil-ak had come for her in the night and carried her away. I didn't believe either of those stories, but I was scared for her and hoped she was all right. On the third day she came

back. The outsiders' boat was gone and it was safe. She later told me that she had run flat out for an entire day before stopping. It then took her two days to walk back to town.

Soon after that, fall crept in swiftly, as it does in in the North, with me very grateful to still be with my family. I watched the slow return of night without speaking very often to anyone except my father—not only because he was the only one who could speak English, but also because he was the only one who understood what I had been through.

Chapter SEVEN

MY FATHER TRIED to keep me busy helping him build our cabin. I had to comb the beach every day to find the logs we needed for each layer of the walls. Then we had to carve the logs precisely to fit them together. Father knew that I was like him and that hard work eased my loneliness and pain.

When I started helping my father, he instructed me mostly in English with some Inuvialuktun mixed in. By the time we began chinking our cabin in the early fall, filling the gaps between the logs, he used our native tongue with bits of English. And by the time our cabin was finished, just after the snows came in September, he asked me to do many of the tasks in straight Inuvialuktun.

I was unsure how I would keep myself busy after our work was done. My mother suggested I make friends, but I didn't fit in and had no idea where to begin. I did see Agnes on occasion and her mother did allow us to speak to one another, now that I had rediscovered my own tongue. But even though she was out of the hospital again, her mother was so ill that Agnes had little time for anything apart from caring for her.

See photo on page 117.

"COME," MY FATHER SAID to me one day in Inuvialuktun, when the sky was still mostly dark. One of his jobs in the winter was to cut chunks of ice from a local lake, to supply drinking water for the missionaries. I loved helping him gather the ice. My canvas shoes had long since become impractical in the harsh Arctic climate, so I pulled on my kamik, put on my parka, and joined him outside by the dogsled.

As we neared the lake where we collected the ice, it was late morning and the sun was just beginning to rise. A shimmer of pale light illuminated the snowy hill between us and the lake. Descending it always scared me, despite my father's ability with the sled, but on this day he stopped when he reached the top and said, "I think I am going to walk from here."

"But what about the sled?" I asked.

He laughed and hopped off. "You'll manage fine," he said over his shoulder.

The dogs moved forward.

"I can't," I cried out. "Help!"

"Just use the brake," he called back.

"I can't," I cried again, trying to move my shaking foot between the runners to press on the brake.

"You can do it. Stop being chicken," he said. It was his favorite English phrase, and while I did not know exactly what it meant, I knew that I had to be brave.

As soon as I reached the bottom, my father ran up to meet me. He grabbed me and kissed my cheek. He smiled. "You handled that like a true Inuk."

When we returned home, he told my mother and siblings all about it, as if I was a great Inuvialuit hero. They were all proud, and I felt Olemaun grow large inside of me.

IN THE WINTER, WE SELDOM went outside, except to visit our neighbors. We spent many hours in our new cabin, which was roomier than the tent. When we did gather with others, I was still nervous about speaking our language with anyone other than my

father, so I learned to listen. The elders talked constantly at these gatherings, and I sat at their feet practicing my beading and doing needlepoint while their words played like music in my head. Day after day

I listened, and over time meaning emerged, rocking me back to remembrance as night settled on us with its darkness and cold.

Agnes came too, when her mother was well enough to leave her home. I cherished just sitting next to her, even if we didn't talk, because as much as we loved each other's company, we did not want to miss a word of the elders' stories.

I still worried for my parents' souls, but as hard as I tried I could not convince them to bring prayer into our home. I understood from the elders that they had their own stories to give them guidance, stories that were handed down instead of being written. But the stories were not about Jesus, and the nuns had taught us that no one could go to Heaven without stories about Jesus.

ONE DAY IN EARLY DECEMBER, my father loaded his sled, hooked up the dogs, and said good-bye to us. He was going to check on people who lived in remote locations, trappers and others. The RCMP hired men like my father, men who knew the land well and were

See photo on page 118.

83

skilled at surviving the dark days and the harsh climate, as special constables.

I was sad to see him go. He was the only one who nurtured Olemaun instead of chastising Margaret. I missed our trips to collect ice and how he would let me drive the dogs. I missed the way he would touch my cheek and smile when he was proud of me. I missed the smell of his pipe smoke. I had only my little brother to play with, because my sisters had quit asking me to join their games. They accepted me when I read aloud to them, but I grew tired of reading the same stories over and over again. I spent a great deal of my time playing string games with Ernest and helping my mother. My Inuvialuktun was improving, but I was still shy about speaking it, and I had already been labeled an outsider, so making friends was not any easier than before.

Some nights I sat at the feet of the elders; others I spent in my new bed reading by lamplight and dreaming of Christmas, when my father would return. I hoped that he would buy me some new books with the money he earned. I had always wondered why

Christmas was so important to my father when we weren't Christians, but after going to the outsiders' school I partly understood. There, it was the only day of the year you weren't woken at an insane hour to do chores, and the outsiders actually gave you enough to eat. They even served it on fancy china dishes.

MY FATHER WAS AWAY for three weeks, which seemed an eternity to me that winter. When he came home, I was in the store trying to decide which books I would like most. High on a shelf, something caught my eye: three lace-covered porcelain dolls unlike any I had ever seen before. They were pale like outsiders, but their wide glass eyes were full of innocence and kindness. Their lips were pursed into little red bows. I stared at them with wonder.

Elizabeth threw open the door, letting in a cold gust of air. "Father has returned. Come!" she said in Inuvialuktun.

I squealed with delight and followed her, running toward home. The icy air stung our lungs in the black afternoon, but we couldn't wait for Father to hold us in his strong arms.

He looked very thin but he wore a big, fat smile. I wrapped my arms around him as tightly as possible, until I felt as if we were one.

After my father had settled in and had a good meal of smoked herring—which I now knew was called pouchiak—he took his dogs and sled down to the Hudson's Bay store. I wanted to go too, to be near him and the dogs, but none of us was allowed to go. We all sat on pins and needles, even my mother, waiting to see what he would bring home. He returned with our presents hidden under the canvas on his sled. We would have to wait another three days.

I could smell warm bannock baking when I woke on Christmas morning. I was still very sleepy, but hunger and curiosity drew me out from under my blankets. I helped my father wake my sisters and my brother. After we were all awake, my father gave my mother a beautiful wooden chest full of eating utensils. They sparkled in the lamplight and looked very expensive. My mother turned them over and over again in her tiny hands. My brother received a toy train made of tin, a train like the ones I had read about in books, the trains that outsiders used instead of dogsleds and boats to travel far distances. Mabel and Elizabeth received the best gifts of all. My father had bought them two of the dolls I had admired only a few days before, the dolls with the fancy dresses and leather shoes.

I waited for him to give me a doll too, but he didn't. He hadn't even bought me a book. My sisters sometimes teased me because they were jealous of the time I spent with our father. They would tell me that I wasn't really part of the family. I had learned to speak some of our language again and my hair had grown longer, but not getting a doll suggested that my sisters could be right. I had thought my father understood me. I cried.

"What is wrong?" my father asked, his voice teasing.

"I wanted a doll, too," I answered through sobs.

"Aren't you too grown-up for dolls?"

I shook my head. "No." The dolls we had made out of scraps at the outsiders' school were clumsy, with lopsided or missing faces, and seldom had hair.

They were nothing like the dolls we saw in books, or
like the ones my sisters held in their arms while they
stared at me.

My father pulled me against him and kissed my
cheek. "Really?"

"Really," I said, leaning my head against his shoulder.

He had a mischievous look in his eyes. "Does that
mean you are too little for your own dogsled?"

I wanted to say something, but I was frozen with
shock. I had to wait a moment, to replay his words
in my head before I could believe them. Then my
tears turned to tears of joy. My father thought I was
grown-up enough to handle my own team! I pulled
on my kamik and parka and ran outside. It was true!
I had my own dogsled, and hitched to it were six
dogs. I scratched each one around its harness. Then I
pulled up the anchor from the snow, tossed it on the
sled, and raced around and around our cabin under
the blue-green fronds of the northern lights. I never
wanted to stop.

See photo
on page 118.

The next day Father and I took our sleds down
through the village. He led me to the Hudson's Bay
Company, where he came to a stop. We went inside

and he let me pick out two books. While I was scanning the titles, I wondered if the Du-bil-ak had taken books from this very shelf with him out to his traplines, as my father had taken the Bible. Reading had certainly helped me and Agnes with our loneliness. I made a mental note to bring more of the books I had already read to the next gathering for Agnes, now that I was getting new ones. I understood how exciting it was to have something fresh to read, though I doubted I would be doing as much reading now that I had my own dogs and sled.

My father took the books to the counter and whispered so low to the clerk that I could not hear what he said. The clerk came out and walked over to the shelf, where I was now admiring the doll. He reached above my head, took it down, and handed it to me. It had to be the very best day of my life! I smiled so hard my cheeks hurt. While my father watched me, I fingered the dark brown curls and lace ruffles and remembered when I had thought the nuns all had such hair under their habits. That was before I had caught a glimpse of a shaved scalp. This doll was nothing like them. She was so beautiful.

I slipped my doll inside my parka and carried her home. My sisters complained and were jealous, until my father gave them each a piece of rock candy. Later, we made little beds for our dolls and pretended they were three sisters who did everything together. We even let our little brother pull them around on his train to exotic, far-off places.

Then my sisters wanted Ernest to pretend that his train was taking them to the outsiders' school. I didn't want to play with them anymore if they were silly enough to think that anything as beautiful as our dolls would ever be seen in a place like that. I didn't tell Mabel and Elizabeth that the nuns would chop off their dolls' pretty ringlets and make them wear shabby clothes that didn't fit properly. I didn't think anyone needed to know about that.

Chapter EIGHT

See photo on page 119.

Near the end of February, when light began popping its head up from the darkness for a brief moment each day like a sik-sik, my father told us to pack for a hunting trip to the Husky Lakes. The Husky Lakes were more like one body of water sprawled out in a tangle. The trip there took two days by dogsled, and I used my own sled the entire time.

We made our camp and settled in for the week. My mother took my sisters to set nets for fishing, and my father took me and Ernest, who was bundled in my father's sled, to hunt for caribou. My father always knew how to find the herd. He was an excellent hunter. He had learned from his grandfather, who was one of the greatest hunters our people had ever known.

I was worried that the hunt might not be successful. My father had worn a pained and troubled look for the entire trip. Something was bothering him, and I thought that maybe the herds would be scarce. But my father always found the tuk-tu, as I now called them again. As we approached them, he motioned for me to pull my sled to a stop. I anchored mine in silence, as my father did his. He crept forward on foot and crouched behind a low rise. As my brother slept, I crept up beside my father.

Tuk-tu

Tuk-tu is the Inuvialuit name for caribou. Tuk-tu travel in herds across the North and are a food staple of the people who live there.

A shot cracked through the air, and then another. My father had managed to drop two animals before the herd scattered across the tundra. He ran toward the downed caribou. Leaving my own sled where it was, I jumped onto my father's sled, where my brother, still bundled tight in furs but startled from his sleep by the shots, was now crying. I shushed him as we flew after our father, and Ernest was asleep again before we reached him.

I stopped the dogs and jumped off the sled, my ulu ready. We had two animals to skin before they froze solid. I had seen my father skin animals many times when I was a young girl, and I had listened intently when the elder women talked of the best way to do so. I was sure I knew exactly how it should be done. And I was right: I made no holes in the hide. My mother would be impressed.

"You have done well, Olemaun. You are a strong child," my father said.

His words floated around inside me. I had made him proud!

My father kept looking at me as we packed the meat onto the sleds. I stood tall, pleased with myself. Then I noticed that his eyes were glassy and wet. He went onto one knee and stroked my face inside the fur trim on my parka. I was confused. Something was wrong.

"What is it?" I asked.

"I'm sorry, Olemaun," he said, his voice cracking.

"But why?"

He couldn't speak for a long time. Finally he cleared his throat. "I am going to ask something very difficult of you. You will need to be brave."

"Sure, Father. What do you need?"

He stared out across the tundra. His eyes could not meet mine. "The government is telling us to send our children to school," he said. He rubbed his face with the palms of his hands, as if he were trying to erase some painful knowledge from his mind. "It was easier to avoid on Banks Island, but here… More of them will be coming. Without learning their language and how to read and write it, we won't survive. The clerk has your mother sign for supplies we did not buy, and

she doesn't know the difference because she can't read."

"But I can read and write," I assured him. "I can help Mother."

My father closed his eyes and hung his head for a moment. "Yes, but your sisters can't." A tremor quaked all through his body. He shook so hard I thought maybe every bone in his body would break.

My eyelashes became sticky with ice. I understood. He was asking me to go with my sisters, to go back to that horrible place. He needed me to protect them.

My father crushed me against his chest, and we both cried until we had no more tears.

I didn't cry again after that. The *Immaculata* would not arrive until late June, but I needed to start preparing myself now to go back. I had to teach myself how not to cry anymore.

MY SISTERS WERE EXCITED when they heard that they would be going to the school like their big sisters. They saw it as a sign of maturity, but I knew it would be better for them to be frozen forever as they were now than to grow up in a place like that. I wanted to tell him how badly I wanted to stay and how I never wanted to leave, but I had to be tough— for my father, who bore a great weight of guilt, for my mother, who was frightened of losing her children, and most of all for my sisters, who would need someone to protect them.

I woke early the morning we were to return to school on the outsiders' boat and packed my things before anyone else awoke. Later, while my sisters packed, Ernest cried. I could not stand to hear it. I went outside and said my good-byes to my dogs.

WHEN WE REACHED the dock, Mabel squeezed my fingers tightly and called me Agun, an affectionate word meaning "big sister." She and Elizabeth had not called me that since I had first left for the school three years earlier. I could feel her shaking. Elizabeth ran ahead of us up the gangway onto the *Immaculata*. She was excited to go to Aklavik. I had once been that excited to go to school. My father hugged me tightly and my mother kissed me. Ernest started to cry.

Just before Mabel and I reached the gangway, my mother pressed a slip of paper into my hand. "Read it later," she whispered.

I tucked it into my kamik and looked to my father. His head hung low. I could not see his face inside the hood of his parka; he was ashamed for asking me to go back to the school.

Both of my sisters wore short bob haircuts. My mother had cut their hair at home to spare them the humiliation of having it done at school. I was now old enough to keep my hair long and had been spared. My stomach felt tight; all of me felt tight.

The girl who had taunted me months before tripped as she stepped onto the plank. I gave her my hand, helping her up from the mucky shore. She managed a slight smile and turned to make her way up the gangway.

As the boat left the dock, I was the only child who did not cry; even Elizabeth burst into tears when the boat started moving. The excitement ran off her face and fell on the deck along with her tears.

All of the children stared at their parents, waving and calling to them. I scanned the crowd for Agnes but saw no sign. She had taken off to hide again. I wished that my sisters and I could have joined her, but they were too eager to learn to read, as I had once been, and there was no convincing them that we would be better off to disappear for a while. I was happy that Agnes had once again gotten away, but I was sorry that I did not get the chance to say good-bye to her. My father later wrote me to tell me that she was again found safe.

I turned away from the shore. I didn't want to remember my mother's face fading from view or my

father's bowed head. I didn't want to lock that memory into my mind.

AS WE LEFT THE SHORE, a flock of geese flew overhead, no question in their minds about where they belonged. I watched them with envy. No one would ask them to fly somewhere other than on their course. And next year, when they returned to their nesting grounds, the other birds who would meet them there would not care where it was they had been for the winter.

See photo on page 119.

The geese disappeared and the mouth of the Mackenzie River Delta swallowed up us weeping children. My sisters clung to me as the *Immaculata* traveled down the intestinal tract of the mainland, far from the warmth of our parents' cheeks and the soft fur of their parkas that we had felt only minutes before.

We passed the supply barge as it approached from upriver. A new tugboat had replaced the paddle wheeler and it guided the barge toward Tuk. My father was right. Things were changing. This new, faster boat was another sign of that. Every child aboard the

Immaculata wished they had the strength to jump
over to that new tugboat and go back to their parents'
open arms. But none of us did, and after a time it was
gone from our sight.

I stared out at the river's edge for a long time,
trying to prepare myself for what waited at the end
of our journey. Mostly I was thinking of how I would
protect my sisters. And then I saw him, off in the
distance, making his way toward Tuk to meet the
supply barge, pelts slung in bales over his shoulders—

the Du-bil-ak. Watching him walk in that grizzly-like manner of his reminded me of how strong a person could really be.

I looked to my sisters. This time would be different. I would have them with me. I would not be alone, though my mother would now be without her daughters for a whole year. That's when I remembered the piece of paper that she had handed me earlier. I pulled it from my kamik and unfolded it. On the paper was written *LENA*, my mother's name, in her own hand. She had written her own name!

I held the paper to my heart. Our journey wasn't going to be an easy one, but we would return, steeped in the outsiders' knowledge and also with the wisdom of our own people. I would make sure my sisters retained that wisdom, and that living with the outsiders would not make them forget what home meant. Home was not only where you were safe but also where your family was, and there was strength in having each other. I was Olemaun now, and I would keep us together, safe and strong. I would teach my

See photo on page 120.

sisters how to ward off the outsiders' spells, the spells that could bind you in something scratchy and thin and tight, like the uniforms they would make us wear, until we no longer knew where we fit in. I would teach my sisters to walk each day of their lives as though they were wearing a warm and beautiful parka, with their heads held high as if they always belonged, no matter where they were.

After THE STORY

I T WAS HARD FOR MY FATHER to ask me to
go back to the school, but he knew he could rely
on me to care for my sisters. Because I was one of
the older girls by then, the nuns picked on me less,
though they still seemed to ask a lot of me. I had
learned a great deal about how the school worked and
what to do to stay out of the nuns' way, and I made
sure that my sisters knew as well.

The long hours of hard work were difficult for
them to adjust to, but it was the homesickness that

was the most unbearable. Sometimes I would wake to find my sisters standing over my bed, crying. I would pull the blankets back and let them crawl in with me, even though it was forbidden (I was punished when I did get caught). I would whisper stories or sing them songs in Inuvialuktun until they fell asleep. It was all I could do to make them feel better. But, as awful as it was, my sisters remained true Pokiaks: strong-willed and determined. Mabel did so well in school that she went on to high school in Yellowknife and eventually trained as a nurse.

See photo on page 120.

The SCHOOLS

A S EUROPEANS SPREAD throughout North America, their quest to expand into new territories led them to seek ways to remove the people who already inhabited the land. One way of doing this was to send Aboriginal children to live at church-run schools, where their traditional skills were replaced by those that would equip them to function in menial jobs. Like many parents, Margaret's parents were torn as they wondered if sending their children to the schools might be necessary in order to prepare them for the rapidly changing world. Most children, however, were forcibly taken, some, even kidnapped by government agents and church authorities.

The schools were extremely effective in attaining their main goal, which was to strip Aboriginal children of their roots. Most suffered upon rejoining their communities, just as Margaret did when she returned from Aklavik. They could no longer speak to even their mothers and fathers, and they had lost the knowledge of the old ways, which was so essential for survival in the North. They came home to the place of their people, but they still had a great distance to cover before they could return to a place of belonging. Those who had not been to the schools couldn't understand the hurdles facing the returning children. They often shunned them and treated them as outsiders, seeing no value in what they had been taught.

Meeting with ostracism when they were expecting a return to safety only added to the wounds that many of the children carried from having been abused at the schools. Some children, like Margaret, fought hard to reclaim their place among their people, while others learned to cope within the margins of their communities. Still others left to find work in the outside world, because they believed it would be easier for them to live there.

Today, many Aboriginal people seek to reclaim their lost ways as a means of unifying and healing their communities. Traditional languages are being offered for study in some schools, elders are being invited to share their knowledge and stories with the younger generations, and culture is being celebrated through powwows, the creation of traditional art and handicrafts, and athletic events such as the Arctic Winter Games. The feelings of shame that have kept so many survivors on the outside of their own communities are being lifted through Truth and Reconciliation Commission national events, healing circles, and residential school reunions, where experiences can be shared in a supportive setting, and through the work of brave survivors like Margaret who have told their stories in all forms of art and media—including books like this one.

Olemaun's SCRAPBOOK

I turned around to look at them where they stood,
perched like birds of prey at the rail of the Immaculata.

We had all waited for so long to be reunited with our parents
in Tuktoyaktuk. The shoreline of Tuktoyaktuk looks quite
different today because the waters have risen so much.

Olemaun's father, Bertram,
and mother, Lena.

When we passed the Hudson's Bay Company store, my mother
asked my father to stop and buy me some of the outsiders' food.

My spirits lifted when we made it to our canvas tent, which was set up on a wooden frame near a small lake a short way past the village. This frame tent is similar to the one that Margaret's family lived in.

There was also a chill in the tent, so I prepared the cook fire, thinking of what I might be able to make that I could stomach. This is what the interior of Margaret's family's tent would have looked like.

In the distance, the massive barge appeared, a stern-wheeler pushing it down the river across the bay toward the bank.

Most men in the North worked as trappers. The man pictured here is taking his fox pelts to the Hudson's Bay Company post for trade.

My father was waiting for us at the site of our new home. The first house that Margaret's father built was bought by the government and torn down. This is the second home he built, which was also bought by the government later and replaced by a school.

My mother took me with her because she could not read and did not trust the clerk at the store.

I saw a picture of Lena Horne when I was at the outsiders' school and she is dark like that.

Margaret's younger brother Ernest, who was known for his big, fat cheeks.

An illustration from the
book *Gulliver's Travels* by
Jonathan Swift, depicting
Gulliver and the inhabit-
ants of Lilliput.

I passed the weeks that followed in solitude, or playing with the dogs.
Families relied heavily on their dogs when dogsleds were the
only available means of rapid land transportation. Today they
use snowmobiles.

*On the day the outsiders' boat came back to gather up children,
I hid under my parents' bed.* The journey to school was a long
one, which meant the children could not return home during
the school year.

*One of [Father's] jobs in the winter was to cut chunks of ice
from a local lake, to supply drinking water for the missionaries.*

The RCMP hired men like my father, men who knew the land well and were skilled at surviving the dark days and harsh climate, as special constables. This man, like Margaret's father, used his traditional knowledge about coping in the extreme environment to aid the RCMP, who were not as well equipped for it.

Then I pulled up the anchor from the snow, tossed it on the sled, and raced around our cabin under the blue-green fronds of the northern lights. The northern lights are moving curtains of light, often green or greenish blue, that appear in the sky near the magnetic North Pole. Most often seen in March and September, their scientific name is aurora borealis.

Near the end of February, when light began popping its head up from the darkness for a brief moment each day like a sik-sik, my father told us to pack for a hunting trip to the Husky Lakes. Margaret's family also traveled across land by dogsled.

The geese disappeared and the mouth of the Mackenzie River Delta swallowed up us weeping children.

Margaret's family. From left to right are her father, holding Boogie; Molly; her mother, holding Frank, with Samantha in front of her; Margaret; and Elizabeth.

Mabel at school in Aklavik.

Acknowledgments

THE AUTHOR WISHES TO thank everyone who helped bring this story to print, including Elizabeth Pokiak-Pertschy, James Pokiak, and Mindy Willet, for their book *Proud to Be Inuvialuit* (Fifth House, 2010), Maggie de Vries, Pam Robertson, and Gillian Watts. Thank you also to Annick Press.

Photo CREDITS

vi: (Margaret and her mother and sisters) courtesy of Elizabeth Pokiak-Pertschy

2: basic map outlines by Map Resources. Additions by Lisa Hemingway.

12: (muktuk) NWT Archives/Dept. of Public Works and Services/G-1995-001: 0540

18: (Delta braid) courtesy of Christy Jordan-Fenton

24: (bannock) © istockphoto.com/Falk Kienas

29: (kamik) courtesy of Christy Jordan-Fenton

40: (sik-sik) © istockphoto.com/Harry Kolenbrander

60 (ulu) © istockphoto.com/choicegraphx

93: (tuk-tu) © istockphoto.com/Andrew Coleman

110: (top, the Immaculata) Library and Archives Canada/PA-101292; (bottom, Tuktoyaktuk) Fleming/NWT Archives/N-1979-050-1082

111: (top, Margaret's father and mother) courtesy of Margaret Pokiak-Fenton; (bottom, Hudson's Bay store exterior) NWT Archives/Terrance Hunt fonds/N-1979-062: 0011

112: (top, tent exterior) R. Knights/NWT Archives/N-1991-073-0013; (bottom, tent interior) R. Knights/NWT Archives/N-1993-002-0192

113: (top, stern-wheeler) NWT Archives/Edmonton Air Museum Committee Collection/N-1979-003: 0539; (bottom, trapper) NWT Archives/Northwest Territories. Dept. of Information fonds/G-1979-023: 1793

114: (top, second home built by Margaret's father) courtesy of Elizabeth Pokiak-Pertschy; (bottom, Hudson's Bay store interior) NWT Archives/Douglas Wilkinson fonds/N-1979-051: 1074

115: (top, Lena Horne) The Kobal Collection; (bottom, Ernest) courtesy of Margaret Pokiak-Fenton

116: (top, from Gulliver's Travels) The Art Archive/Kharbine-Tapabor; (bottom, dogs) NWT Archives/Douglas Wilkinson fonds/N-1979-051: 0857S

117: (top, leaving for school) NWT Archives/Terrance Hunt fonds/N-1979-062: 0072; (bottom, cutting ice) NWT Archives/Northwest Territories. Dept. of Information fonds/G-1979-023: 0927

118: (top, RCMP special constable) NWT Archives/Northwest Territories. Dept. of Information fonds/G-1979-023: 2292; (bottom, northern lights) NWT Archives/Northwest Territories. Dept. of Public Works and Services fonds/G-1995-001: 8015

119: (top, dogsled) R. Knights/NWT Archives/N-1993-002-0223; (bottom, Mackenzie Delta) NWT Archives/Northwest Territories. Dept. of Information fonds/G-1979-023: 2405

120: (top, Mabel in Aklavik) courtesy of Margaret Pokiak-Fenton; (bottom, Pokiak family) NWT Archives/Holman Photohistorical and Oral History Research Committee/N-1990-004: 0068

110-120: (background) © istockphoto.com/Peter Zelei

CHRISTY JORDAN-FENTON has been an infantry soldier, a pipeline laborer, a survival instructor, and a bareback bronco rider. Christy has also worked with street children. She was born just outside of Rimbey, Alberta, and has lived in Australia, South Africa, and the United States. Christy now lives on a farm near Fort St. John, British Columbia, where she and her husband are raising three small children, a few chickens, three dogs, a llama, two rabbits, and enough horses to outfit an entire town. Christy worked with her mother-in-law, Margaret Pokiak-Fenton, to write this story. This is the second story that they've written together.

Margaret and her husband, Lyle, 1962.

MARGARET POKIAK-FENTON was born on a tiny island far north of the Arctic Circle. She spent her early years on Banks Island; when she was eight years old she traveled to the mainland to attend the Catholic residential school in Aklavik, Northwest Territories. In her early twenties, while working for the Hudson's Bay Company in Tuktoyaktuk, she met her husband-to-be, Lyle, who was working on the dew Line project. She followed him south to Fort St. John and together they raised eight children. Margaret can be found most Saturdays at the local farmers' market, where she sells traditional Inuit crafts and the best bread and bannock in the North Peace.

Liz at 10 years old

LIZ AMINI-HOLMES was born and raised in the San Francisco Bay area, Liz painted and drew as a child, but she was also interested in becoming an archeologist, a paranormal researcher, an astronaut, and a detective with Scotland Yard. However, she decided that working as an artist was way more fun than any of those jobs and required a lot less math. Liz creates illustrations for books, editorial, advertising, merchandising, and multimedia. In her spare time she reads several books at once, writes fiction, cooks up new recipes, and gets into mischief. She is very ticklish, laughs in the face of danger, and prides herself on not taking anything too seriously!